Pretty Amazing

HOW I FOUND MYSELF IN THE DOWNTOWN EASTSIDE

by

TERESA HEARTCHILD

Revised and Updated, 2024 (with Teresa Heartchild)
First Printing, 2016

Title: Pretty Amazing: How I Found Myself in the Downtown Eastside
ISBN: 978-1-9994061-9-6

Publisher: The James Gang, Iconoclasts Inc., Vancouver, BC, Canada

www.teresaheartchild.com

CONTENTS

FROM COCOON TO BUTTERFLY

Introduction by Franke James

What does Vancouver's Downtown Eastside look like through the eyes of an artist—an artist who also happens to have Down syndrome? Teresa Heartchild's colourful art and poetry let's us see, hear and feel it from her unique viewpoint.

Pretty Amazing: How I Found Myself in the Downtown Eastside is a collection of art and poetry that shows us what Teresa cares about. She has mapped out the neighbourhood as she sees it. Her favourite coffee shop is Prado. She shops for groceries at Nesters and Costco. She loves to visit Gallery Gachet, London Drugs, Top of Vancouver, Woodwards and the Flying Pig. From our home in Gastown, she watches the big cargo ships, like Hanjin, Hapag-Lloyd and Hyundai sailing into the Port of Vancouver. All of these elements combine to create her distinctive visual and poetic vocabulary.

But the heart of *Pretty Amazing* is the unexpected story of Teresa finding herself as an artist and poet. Previously, Teresa's artistic expression was discouraged and ridiculed. But here in the Downtown Eastside, she has found her voice. Her opening poem, *I Am Alive*, packs added punch when you know that her future was written off a few years ago when she lived in Ontario.

In 2013, Teresa was forced into an Ontario nursing home against her will. The Ontario health-care system had wrapped her in, as disability advocate Paul Young says, "a cocoon of impossibility". Against her wishes, Teresa's liberty and freedom was traded for a single bed in an end-of-life nursing home. It was a violation of her human rights. She did not want to be there. Teresa had things to do, places to go, and people to meet!

Fortunately, Teresa's father (a retired lawyer) was able to secure her discharge. The next day Teresa came to live with me and my husband. Three months later, we moved from Ontario to British Columbia and eventually settled in Vancouver.

Teresa is one of the few people to get their freedom back after being put in long-term care. News reports in The New York Times, CBC Radio, and Institution Watch document the sad truth that thousands of young and middle-aged people with developmental disabilities are wrongly being segregated from society by being put into nursing homes.

Teresa continues to feel the fallout from her experience of being forced into the nursing home. She expresses her worries in her art and "self-talk" poetry. Her poems reflect the dialogue she has with herself. Often, she takes on the role of her own parent saying, "Please be nice to my daughter." And she encourages herself, "You're not afraid of those monsters. You have the power of attorney." (Her power of attorney document helped win her release from the nursing home. To this day, Teresa carries the updated document with her wherever she goes.)

The Schedule is a poem that reveals how Teresa organizes her day. She plans exactly when she's going to have breakfast, lunch, snack and dinner. Her drawings often incorporate numbers, which represent the times of the day. We hear her sense of humour and wordplay when she writes, "We are quite a pair. Eat your pears at Nesters. I love Perrier." When she recites the poem she laughs at her own cleverness.

Teresa has found her voice in the Downtown Eastside. It is a voice that talks about feeling "butterflies", but still finds the courage to fly. Teresa has, in her own words, been "reborn in Gastown."

Franke James is Teresa Heartchild's sister and winner of the
Liberty Award for Excellence in the Arts, BC Civil Liberties Association.

I AM ALIVE

Hello.

Be nice to everyone.

Look, I am alive.

You have to be nice.

I am doing fine.

Thank goodness.

I have to be nice to them.

And to the others.

That's a brilliant idea!

You're thinking.

And I'm thinking too.

I think we need to make a list of the things we need.

Right. I'm alive. Nesters. Flying Pig. Prado.

We love it here.

Everybody loves me.

You guys are alright, I know.

You guys, I am born. I am alive.

Redeemed.

Okay, I am reborn.

In Gastown.

chickenpie
HuNGRY

630 700 730 800
800 830 900 930 1000 1030
1100 1130 1200 12 30 100 130 2002
100 130 200 230 300 330 400 4
500 530
600 630 700 730
800 830 900 930 1000 1030

1100 1130
1200 12 30

THE SCHEDULE

Coffee, breakfast, lunch, and supper.

Six and seven. Eight and nine. Nine and ten. Eleven and twelve.

I want breakfast, lunch and snack, and supper.

Six and seven. Seven and eight. Eight and nine. Nine and ten. Eleven and twelve.

I think we have to have our lunch.

And you love chicken pie.

And cranberry sauce.

Six and seven. Eight and eight. Nine and ten. Eleven and twelve.

We have to have our lunch.

You want a cup of tea? Or orange juice?

I want my lunch.

You are perky.

I am perky.

You are weird.

So are you.

Well, we're quite a pair.

Eat your pears at Nesters.

I love Perrier.

The Surgeons
S. Pocock Teresa

cast

Diet Juice cramberry

Diet CRAM-berry Juice

HASTINGS AND ABBOTT

To Hastings and Abbott.

I have to go to Hastings and Abbott.

My daughter has a heart murmur.

I want to stay up here.

We don't want my daughter out there.

So much for Hastings and Abbott.

We don't want to upset my daughter.

The reason I have to go out.

My daughter has to go out to Hastings and Abbott.

I like chocolate cake.

My daughter wants to go to Nesters and Prado.

Hastings and Abbott.

Okie dokie.

That's a good idea!

We'll have a cappuccino.

And chocolate cake.

NC) Baats Ippy Award

Hampage Lloyd

P-A-Chicken

Hyundai

HASSting Abbot st
I wenTo Teresa
Nesters ANDPRADO
we had a Capp. AND Pocock
Chocolatecake.

VVORDS
WORDS
Hungry yes
Teresa Pocock

COffee

BLUE
chicken Cardon
pies

BirDS

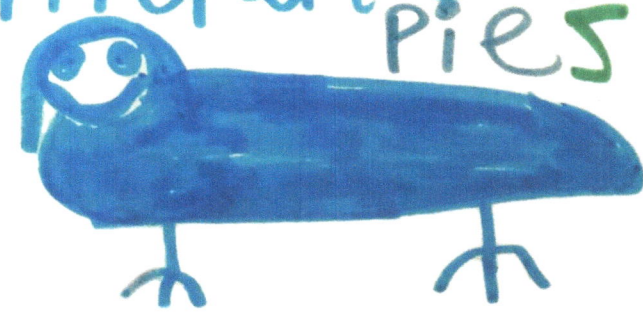

VANCOUVER SUN

I'm doing my work. I'm organizing and those kind of things. I think...

Let me speak. Let me speak. I want to protect the building.

Oh I see. Alright you guys.

Please protect the building. Okay?

We are living in Vancouver and Gastown.

You have to be nice to my daughter. Please be nice to my daughter.

Okay I'll be nice.

The reason my daughter... because she wants to protect the building.

We love Abbott Street. Vancouver.

Okay, because it's not particularly funny.

I know. Well...

The reason she loves Abbott, she loves Vancouver. Please be nice to my daughter.

Okay.

Please be nice to my daughter. Please protect the building. You don't want to upset Abbott.

We don't want to upset the building.

Please be nice to my daughter.

Okay.

Protect my daughter. My daughter needs to calm down.

Okay. She needs to calm down.

Protect the building.

We have more fun here.

00 730 800 830 900 930 1000 1030

00 1130 1200 1230 Pie Chicken

0 130 200 230 300 330 400 430 500 530

00 630 700 730 800 830 E ——————

00 930 1000 1030 1100 1130 1200 1230 E

Juice Diet cranberr

The Vancouver

Sun

THF
Sick
child

0

CRANBERRY Jana

MON

COSCO   PRADO

WED   WED

   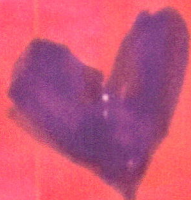

ChocolAtecake

 RaspberryBar

PRADO Thankyou

 TeresaPocock

HAPPY NICE

 RAinbow

I LOVE

COFFEE

LondonDrugs
PRApO

RAINBOW

DOWN SYNDROME DAY

music

Looking glass

WINDWARING

WIND WARNING

I'm afraid to go outside.

There's a wind warning.

I'm afraid to get soaking wet.

I know what you mean.

I'm too chicken and the chickens are very tired.

The wind warning is in the background falling.

Don't frighten me.

Blowing winds and showers.

Oh I see.

Now you're afraid.

I'm afraid of…

It's okay, don't be scared of the showers. You can take an umbrella.

Now that's a brilliant idea. My coat is red. My umbrella is red.

It's okay to go outside. Don't worry.

I do like to sit outside.

We see a big rainbow after the shower.

And the fireworks are beautiful. That's it.

London Drugs
Nestors
Roast Chicken

Chicken Macroi

Rainbows

 COFFEE

 ARTONO

ThFSKchBCDAY

STARWARS

Nursinghome Teres Pococ

The Hospital FACE
FOR Sick Kids books
book knowLedge

THOSE MONSTERS

You're not afraid of those monsters.

I'm going to tell them that I have power of attorney.

You have the power of attorney.

Because we're not scared of monsters.

And that's why... Now, we're even.

Okay, okay, you don't need to be scared of monsters.

And no more complaining.

I know, sorry about that.

Not scared of monsters.

And, I have to be quiet, okay?

We have to be nice to everyone, okay?

Because this is in...

This is in the city of Hastings and Abbott.

I was waiting.

We don't want to hurt their feelings.

Thanks, that was beautiful.

800   900   1000 1100   1200
830   930   1030 1130   1230

⊟⊟⊟▷ 100 130 200 230
        300 330
        400 430 500 53

♡ ♡ ♡ ♡ ♡ ♡   1100
                    1130
                    1200
                    1230

gas Town	cosco chick enpie	Nesters	Land on Drugs	PRADO	The Flying PIG
DAVID Tea	DAVID Coffee	The City Top of VANcouver		THF Sick ch	UBC
ARTONO		TD BANK		WOOD WORDS	
Revam	BCLA		TeResA Pocock		
		UVIC			

University

YOU'RE FIERCE

Music, chicken pie and cranberry sauce.

I don't want to hurt my daughter's feelings.

What?

Now I think I know what it is. Just remain quiet.

Okay.

Quiet, quiet down.

Are you trying to be funny?

It's okay. Calm down.

You're acting funny. My daughter is afraid.

Don't be afraid.

No, there's a monster out there.

Stay calm. I know, you're nervous.

She wants to go back to bed.

Just calm down, my daughter.

We have to have our breakfast, lunch and snack. We have to have chicken pie, cranberry sauce and pasta. But we shouldn't complain.

But there is only one problem. My daughter is afraid.

Oh dear, there is a monster out there.

Right, just stay calm.

Oops.

Now just quiet down. Remain calm.

I want to warn you. I don't want my daughter angry.

Have a shower later on. Cause Woodwards is calling us.

I know, I know.

You got feelings. Relax your stomach. You'll be okay. You're fierce.

Thank you.

RED camera
Computer
CRSauce

Chicken pie
Music
The Internet
monster
Teresa Pocock
BLACKcamera
Abbot street

GOOD FOR THE BODY

It's not that far. You like to walk.

It's only a carrot cake.

It's not that far. Are you crazy?

I'm not going for that. No... I'm 117 pounds.

You need the exercise.

No, I'm too chicken.

I don't think she wants to have cake.

But I am a woman. I don't want to go.

You have to get out to walk.

Everybody needs to walk.

Hey, you're a child. I thought that you liked to walk?

No thank you.

You don't need to worry about it. It is walking. It will make you feel better.

Okay.

Now make up your mind.

I don't want a dilemma.

If we don't get out of here, there's no Prado.

I love Prado.

Give yourself a second chance.

I don't know.

Walking is good for the body.

L DR

PRADO

WOOD
WARD

Gastown

Perrier

ARTono

Chees
e

THSK
ch_

WE LOVE IT HERE

You love it here.

We got a king bed. A queen bed. A nice floor. We love it here.

Between Hastings and Abbott.

We can sit on the patio. We can see cruise ships and Yang Ming and Hyundai.

You can make roasted chicken and cherry tomatoes.

And I love playing scrabble and doing my yoga.

We got everything here.

Look at the restaurants we've got. The restaurants. We love it here.

We got Prado and Flying Pig and London Drugs and Revamped.

We love it here.

You love "Lean on Me".

And "Girls Just Want to Have Fun".

Gastown is fun.

Yeah, you're right, we love it here.

Because of the neighbourhood.

We love it here.

BUTTERFLIES

I got butterflies.

You were a little bit nervous.

They fly around in circles.

You had butterflies on the airplane.

They land inside my stomach.

Flying to Montreal.

I'm afraid of heights.

Speaking at the conference.

I was a little bit nervous.

The Canadian Down Syndrome conference.

But I did it on my own.

That was a good one.

I told them my pretty amazing story.

I think you made your point.

I love my human rights. I like to be nice to everyone.

No wonder you are popular.

Thank you, cause I'm very perky.

You're weird, but you're beautiful.

I want to give all my friends a big H-U-G.

You are amazing.

My feet went happy happy.

Much better.

I am a butterfly!

me

Prado IN GASTOWN

Rainbow

Jung le mouth

ILLUSTRATIONS & PHOTOS

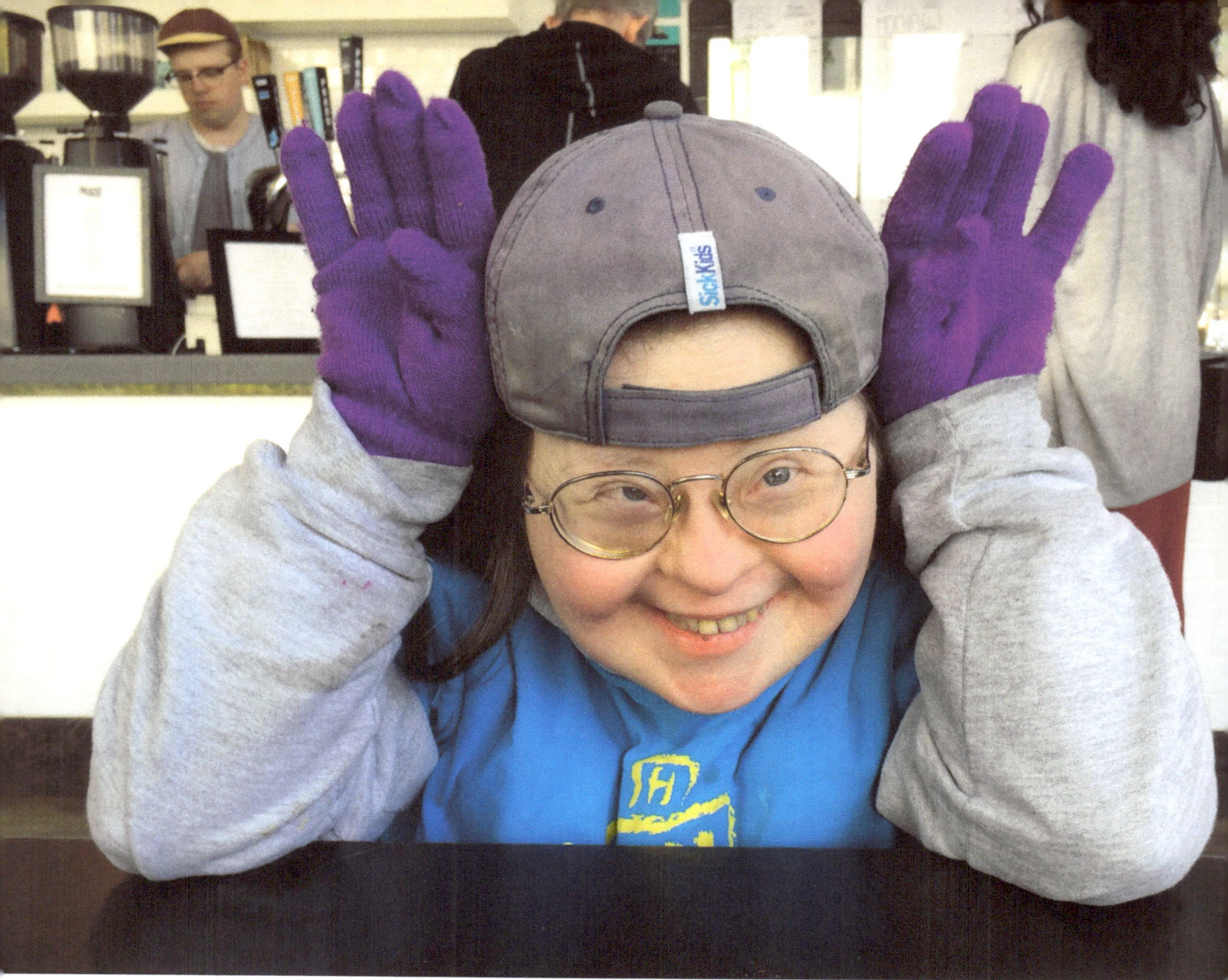

ABOUT TERESA HEARTCHILD

Teresa Heartchild is an artist and poet living in the Downtown Eastside of Vancouver. As a self-advocate with Down syndrome, Teresa presented her story, *I Love My Human Rights*, at the 2016 Canadian Down Syndrome Conference in Montreal. She is a winner of a DTES Small Arts Grant from the Vancouver Foundation which enabled her to create this book.

Teresa is a member of the BC Civil Liberties Association, Gallery Gachet, Inclusion BC, Family Support Institute of BC, and the Canadian Down Syndrome Society. She loves chicken pie, word play and spotting the big boats in the Burrard Inlet.

Ear.
Lotion

ease

Teresa Heartchild in Vancouver